He Looks Too Happy to Be an Assistant Professor

W9-DCC-694

He Looks Too Happy
to Be an Assistant Professor

A Collection of Cartoons

Vivian Scott Hixson

University of Missouri Press   Columbia and London

LIBRARY
ST. LOUIS COMMUNITY COLLEGE
AT FLORISSANT VALLEY

Cartoons copyright © 1985–1995 by Vivian Scott Hixson
Foreword copyright © 1996 by
The Curators of the University of Missouri
University of Missouri Press, Columbia, Missouri 65201
Printed and bound in the United States of America
All rights reserved
5 4 3 2 1   00 99 98 97 96

Library of Congress Cataloging-in-Publication Data

Hixson, Vivian Scott.
He looks too happy to be an assistant professor :
a collection of cartoons / Vivian Scott Hixson.
p.   cm.
ISBN 0-8262-1076-7 (alk. paper)
1. Universities and colleges--United States–Faculty–Caricatures and cartoons.
2. American wit and humor, Pictorial.   I. Title.
NC 1429.H538A4 1996
741.5'973–dc20   96-2306
CIP

∞™ This paper meets the requirements of the
American National Standard for Permanence of Paper
for Printed Library Materials, Z39.48, 1984.

Publication of this book has been assisted by a contribution
from the *Chronicle of Higher Education*.

Foreword
David L. Lendt

William Marcy "Boss" Tweed in 1871 demanded of his henchmen that they "Stop them damn pictures." He was tired of cartoons in *Harper's Weekly* depicting him as the ringleader of an unprincipled gang responsible for looting the public treasury. He lamented that, although his constituents couldn't read, they could "see pictures."

Illiteracy is not, presumably, a problem for the audience of Vivian Scott Hixson, whose cartoons spoof the inhabitants of American institutions of higher education. Faculty, administrators, and students—and those related to them—can best appreciate her knowledge and understanding of the academy, warts and all. Only a grim few would suggest that anyone stop these pictures.

The cartoon form, which took root in the eighteenth century in England, was characterized from the beginning by a combination of caricature and satire. The word, however, was not used to describe such works until 1843. *Cartoons*, in England until that time, described sketches done in preparation of finished paintings or frescoes. When the British government presented an exhibition of cartoons, commissioned for addition to the decor of Parliament, the humor magazine *Punch* ridiculed the event. Convinced there were better uses for public money, the magazine published a sketch of a ragged assemblage of citizens inspecting a gallery of paintings and added the words, "The poor ask for bread and the philanthropy of the State accords an exhibition." *Punch* labeled the drawing "Cartoon No. 1," effectively redefining the word.

Cartoonist Hixson, a sociologist, has taken up a medium of expression dominated by practitioners without formal training in the arts. John James Mitchell, one of the founders of the original *Life* magazine and himself a cartoonist, considered that an advantage. "It is a melancholy fact," he stated in 1889, "that the tendency of an artistic education is to tone down and frequently eliminate, in a majority of students, that playfulness and fancy which are often the very life of a drawing." Trained in the arts or not, the effective cartoonist artfully takes the viewer from familiar to unknown territory. Thus, the skilled cartoonist is also a skilled teacher.

As one of a large band of part-time, temporary professors and the spouse of a history professor, Ms. Hixson enjoys the perspective of a collegiate "insider." Yet, other connections and vantage points reveal to her the tendency of some in the professoriate to isolate themselves and to take themselves, their colleagues, and their work a bit too seriously—and for some students to take their work not seriously enough.

She deflates the academic windbags and points the finger at meddling and officious administrators, misguided students, faculty pettiness, and academic resistance to change. She also uses humor to bring greater understanding to such serious issues as the plight of junior and part-time faculty members and graduate assistants, the litigious atmosphere in which colleges and universities are forced to function, the difficulty of defining a good teacher (and good teaching), and the effects of the pressure to publish.

There was a time when the daily "political cartoon" was one of the most powerful forces in informing and shaping American opinion and policy. Early in this century, the nation's major newspapers "owned" their political cartoonists and were identified with them. Cartoonists whose work was syndicated to hundreds of the nation's daily papers were conspicuous, front-page participants in the most pervasive medium of mass communication. Some enjoyed recognition and rewards commensurate with those of today's network anchors. It could be argued that their line drawings had more political influence than the carefully wrought words on their newspapers' editorial pages. Even subscribers capable of reading might more quickly get the editorial point through the "shorthand" of an incisive political cartoon. As a result, presidents were known to demand, in effect, that someone "Stop them damn pictures."

J. N. "Ding" Darling, one of the most durable, successful, and powerful of cartoonists, was nevertheless aware of the limits of his medium. In a speech in 1928, near the zenith of his career, he said, "A cartoonist may only play upon and reflect the things and emotions that are already before the public. He cannot successfully introduce new topics nor through his medium alone follow through with a process of reasoning. The cartoon is essentially a spotlight service. So it happens that he must be content to play his calcium ray upon the marionettes that strut the visible stage."

While preponderant and growing percentages of Americans accept the view of the world portrayed on their television screens, the art of cartooning remains vigorous and, like the print publications in which cartoons appear, more specialized.

Ms. Hixson's graphic observations are clever and whimsical. They are—in the best cartooning tradition—playful, perceptive, and pointed. They cast a bright light on the marionettes who strut the academic stage. And, except for those in which we stuffy academics might discover ourselves, they are entertaining.*

*An excellent survey of cartooning can be found in Stephen Hess and Milton Kaplan, *The Ungentlemanly Art: A History of American Political Cartoons* (New York: Macmillan Co., 1968, 1975).

Preface

Based on my own experiences and the collective insights of innumerable colleagues and friends, these cartoons spring from the frustrating, the absurd, and the just plain silly situations that we all confront and somehow survive during every day at work in the academic world.

In "normal" life, I am a sociologist; as a "normal" scholar, I should have been converting all these insights into sociological research and analysis. But instead, for better or worse, for richer or poorer (most probably, for poorer), they emerged as cartoons.

In this enterprise, I have been steadily supported by the *Chronicle of Higher Education;* very few of these cartoons would have been created or published without the early and continuing support of Peter Stafford and the rest of the *Chronicle* staff. If I were to thank everyone who has contributed to this collection in any way, the list would go on forever, but no one has been a richer source of trenchant observations than my husband of thirty years, the historian William B. Hixson, Jr., who probably should be listed as a contributing author to the vast majority of the "tag lines" in this book.

He Looks Too Happy to Be an Assistant Professor

"OK. The modern philosophy job. Candidate #1 giggles, candidate #2 is a sloppy eater, and we've eliminated candidate #3 because his advisor wrote a snotty review of Professor Phinney's book. Is there anybody left?"

1

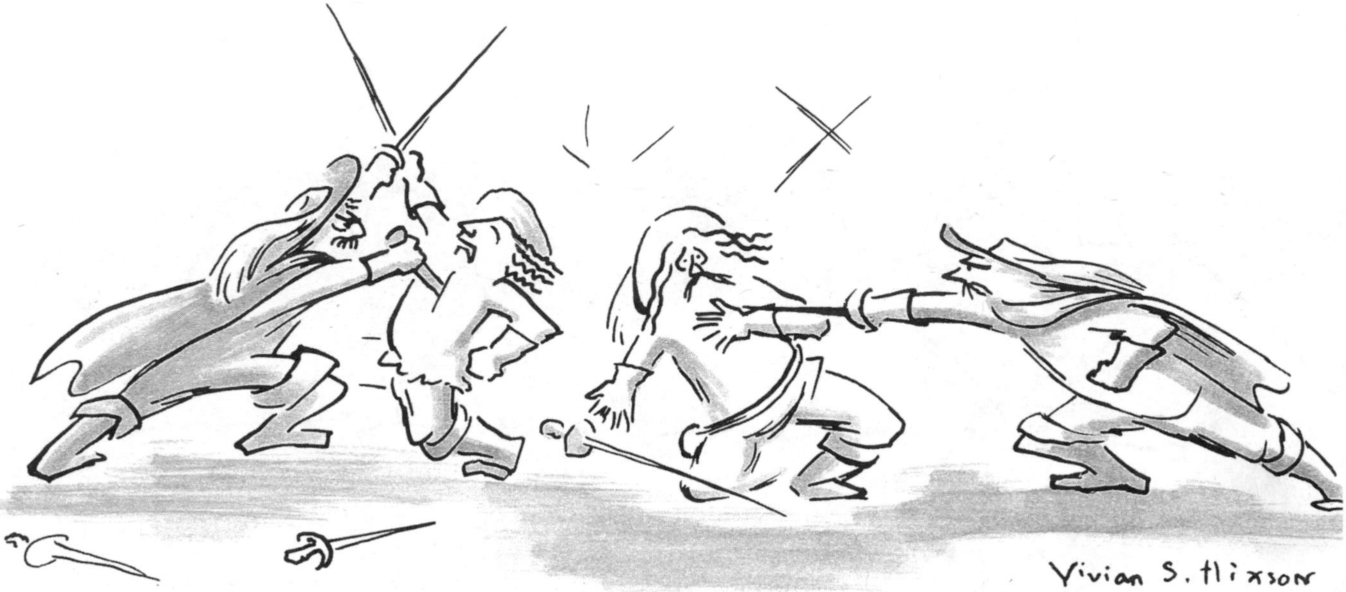
Vivian S. Hixson

Department meeting.

"Bad news. Our money for appointments has been withdrawn. I'm afraid that will leave your committee with nothing to do this year."

"Hey, I've got it! The perfect formula! We put two full professors on the committee to give it clout, and a new assistant professor on so the work will get done."

VS Hixson

"I don't think we're going to get a quorum for the meeting. Professor Schmidt is having a fit of melancholia, Professor Haviland's dog is sick, and the dean has already bought tickets for South Padre Island."

"This is it. The vote is against granting tenure. George will contact our lawyers, Anne will tap the university emergency contingency fund, and I'll hit the newspapers with our side of the story first."

"You're going to *Taiwan* for your sabbatical? But the department can't afford long-distance calls to Taiwan. How will you do your committee work?"

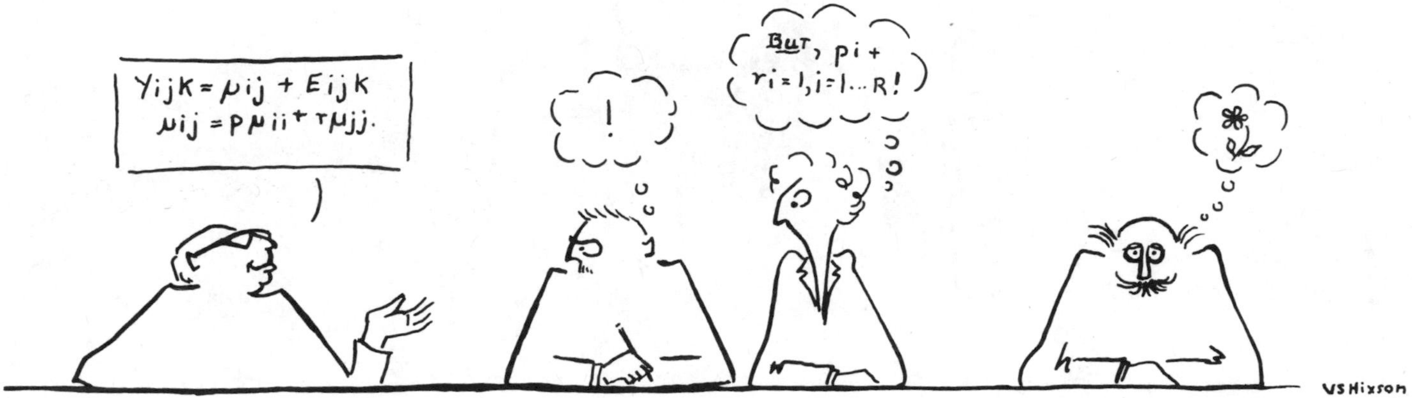
Yijk = μij + Eijk
μij = ρμii + τμjj.
!
But, ρi + τi = 1, i = 1...R!
VSHixson

"Great news! They've certified that we're drug free and that we haven't embezzled federal funds. With that in hand, I think they'll forget about that academic accreditation thing."

Vivian S. Hixson

"It's the new University Redevelopment, Reorganization, and Revitalization plan. What it really means is that we cut staff."

"When the clerk-typists struck, everything was under control, but when the administration tried to draft the faculty to replace them . . ."

"It doesn't really matter exactly how much each person's salary actually *is*. You just have to convince each one of them that he's making a little bit more than the *others* are."

"What this department needs is higher morale. What I mean is that all those egocentric prima donnas have got to stop being so negative about each other."

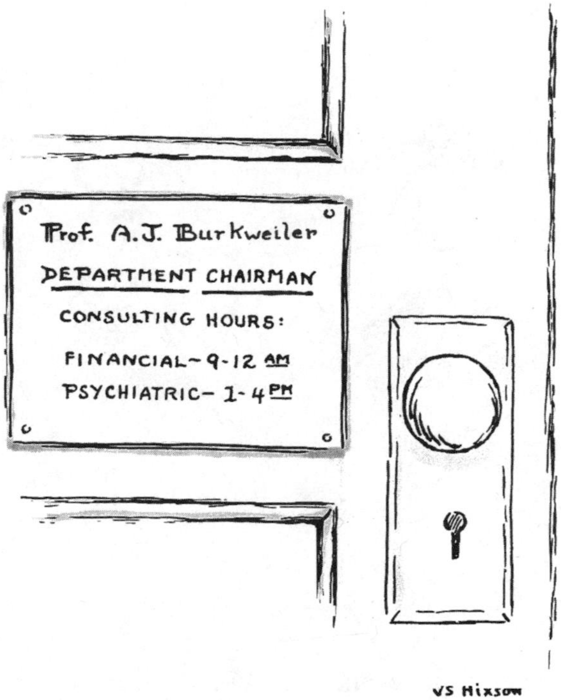
Prof. A.J. Burkweiler
DEPARTMENT CHAIRMAN
CONSULTING HOURS:
FINANCIAL – 9-12 AM
PSYCHIATRIC – 1-4 PM
VS Hixson

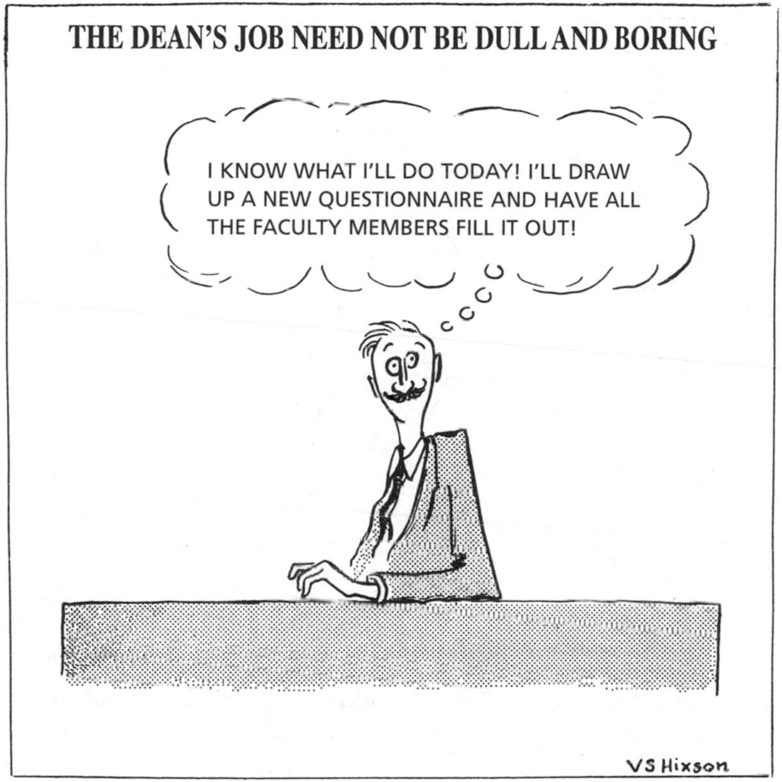
I KNOW WHAT I'LL DO TODAY! I'LL DRAW UP A NEW QUESTIONNAIRE AND HAVE ALL THE FACULTY MEMBERS FILL IT OUT!
VS Hixson

THE DEAN'S JOB NEED NOT BE DULL AND BORING

"Why don't I have clear and definite rules? Because rigid, authoritarian management is out, and flexible, democratic management is in. Besides, if I had clear and definite rules, every time I made a decision, some amateur lawyer on the faculty would haul out the rule book and give me an argument."

"Hey, look. It's really simple. All we do is make a list of all the things we *don't* like to do, and that becomes the new administrator's job definition. Right?"

"This is drops and adds. Grievances and lawsuits is that line, over there."

"George would make a great department chairperson. He's the only one in the department who could plaster and paint the walls *and* repair the office furniture!"

"Women are always complimenting me on my great Affirmative Action hiring record, but the truth is, I don't *like* men."

VSHixson

Dean Anna Methusela discovering that her plan for undergraduate education
(circa 1923) has finally been put into practice.

"Well, yes, we do have a home in Westchester and a vacation house in the Hamptons, but I didn't put that in the financial report because it isn't *liquid*, you see. It isn't *income*."

"I've got it! We make a plan to beef up campus security, and then slip higher-education funding in with the crime bill!"

"Big-time baseball players, bosses in business, TV stars—I'm against pay raises for *all* the fat cats. But I can't vote against *them*, so I'm axing the teachers."

"All right! We'll have that conference, and we *will* stay within budget.
It's simple; we'll all stay in the undergraduate dorms!"

"I presume you realize that your first duty as medieval historian
will be to take part in our door-to-door fund-raiser?"

CREATIVITY IN THE STATE FUNDING CRISIS

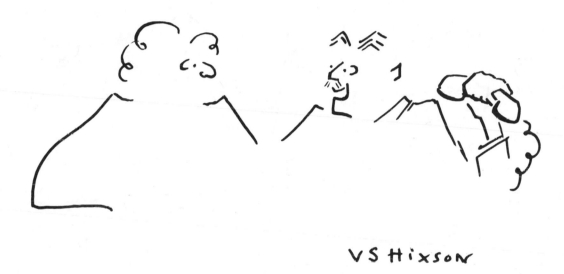

VS Hixson

"OK! If we give Ag. and Tech. University a word processor, they'll
give us two veterinarians and a hybrid avocado!"

"And with this new addition to our library staff, I think we can finally settle that cockroach problem in the all-night reading room."

"We are faced with imminent catastrophe. If this university can't come up with another million dollars, we will definitely—not possibly, but definitely—lose a winning football coach."

VS Hixson

"Ask him for it now. He just got the funds for the academic year, and he's still under the illusion that we'll come out ahead."

"You have an endowed chair? Ha! Useless! *I* have an endowed *parking* place!"

"Look! If we tilt the windows just a bit further to the South, we can raise the interior temperature to 90 degrees!"

Utopia College successfully converts from automobiles to ecologically sound bicycle traffic.

CAMPUS BUILDINGS

English/History/Philosophy. Converted women's dorm, circa 1860. Perpetual steam heat (winter and summer).

Engineering. Will withstand 9.9 on the Richter Scale. No women's rest rooms.

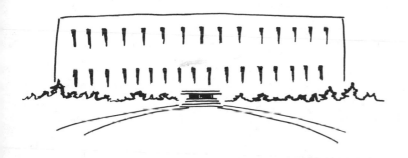

VS HIXSON

Administration Building. Closely resembles a computer data card. Excellent lines of sight in all directions. Underground escape tunnels.

Designed and donated by a generous alumnus. Function unknown.

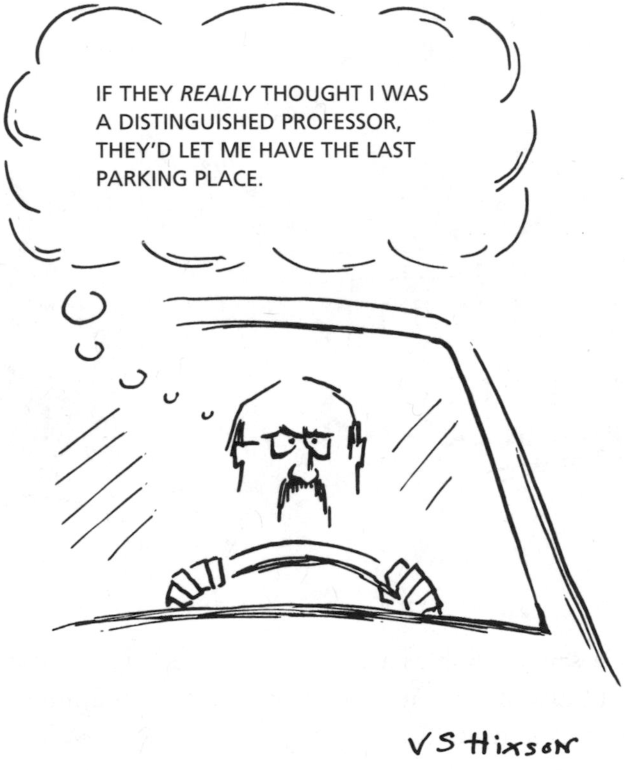
IF THEY *REALLY* THOUGHT I WAS A DISTINGUISHED PROFESSOR, THEY'D LET ME HAVE THE LAST PARKING PLACE.
VS Hixson

DREAMS OF ACADEMIC GLORY

"Dear Professor Hummel:
Not only have we awarded you a grant, but we have decided that your
beautifully written grant application is publishable as it stands."

VS Hixson

"My peace-activist self is delighted that the Star Wars boondoggle
is dying, but my researcher self is in agony."

"I am applying for this grant so that I can get released time from teaching so that I can apply for a larger grant so that . . ."

"Did I understand you to say that, if we hired you, you would be bringing in to the department a grant of some one million dollars?"

The start of a great book.

"I was going to do a research project this summer, but then when I realized that the research project would be six months long, and the summer was only two months long, I decided to go to the beach instead."

"What I'm suggesting is a research partnership. I'll think up the bright ideas, and you'll do the research."

"I love *talking* about research. It's *doing* it that I don't like."

"Well, I don't have any real *evidence* that he's goofing off, but if you ask me, he looks too happy to be an assistant professor."

"So you have a motivation problem. So next time, just make sure you're doing research on something that you really care about."

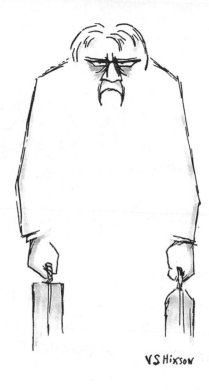

Professor Zack returns from a sabbatical in England, France, and Italy, equipped with a refreshingly new perspective on his position at Midsouthern University.

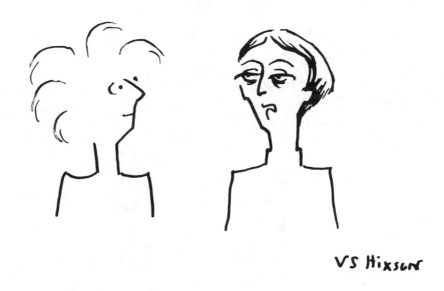

"I'm not a research professor. I'm a research assistant. Research professors get paid. Research assistants do it for the sheer love of learning."

Summary Research

Geology

Biology

Botany

V S Hixson

"I have not written anything this year. I have been too busy filling out the Research and Publication form, the Self-Evaluation form, the Merit Raise form, the Departmental Service form, the . . . "

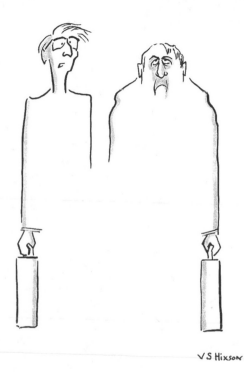

"What it all comes down to is that I'm willing to go through all this crap just on the off chance that some day I'll have the reputation and respect that you have now."

The social psychologist at a cocktail party.

"I just read here that Freud *can* be replicated. Do you think that's true?"

"The great thing about being a psychologist is that you always know *why* you're making a fool of yourself."

INGREDIENTS:
THE NEW YORK TIMES
THE WALL STREET JOURNAL

Vivian S. Hixson

"I don't really need to write a *book* to get promoted. All I need is something in a hard cover with my name on the outside."

"For years I thought he was a professor. Now it turns out he just takes them around to the other side of the stacks and builds play forts out of them."

"You don't mean the library wants them *back*, do you?"

"I'm writing a book predicting the destruction of the atmosphere. Of course, I'm hoping that it *won't* be destroyed; but then, if it is, at least my book will sell."

"Do you think I'll ever be a *beautiful* writer, like you?"

"Actually, I'm *not* the muse of creative writing; I'm the muse of *memory*. But if the people who are going to read this don't know the original sources, I'll do just as well."

Vivian Scott Hixson

"It juxtaposes hegemonic discourse and submergent mentalités, and posits the imminent destruction of das Einfühlen. What I'm really saying is that contemporary literary criticism has lost touch with the masses."

"When I said, 'Give the manuscript a critical reading,' I didn't mean a *critical* reading."

"Good heavens, do you realize what we've just discovered? You and I are the only human beings in existence who are using the English language correctly!"

Two scholars collaborating on a manuscript.

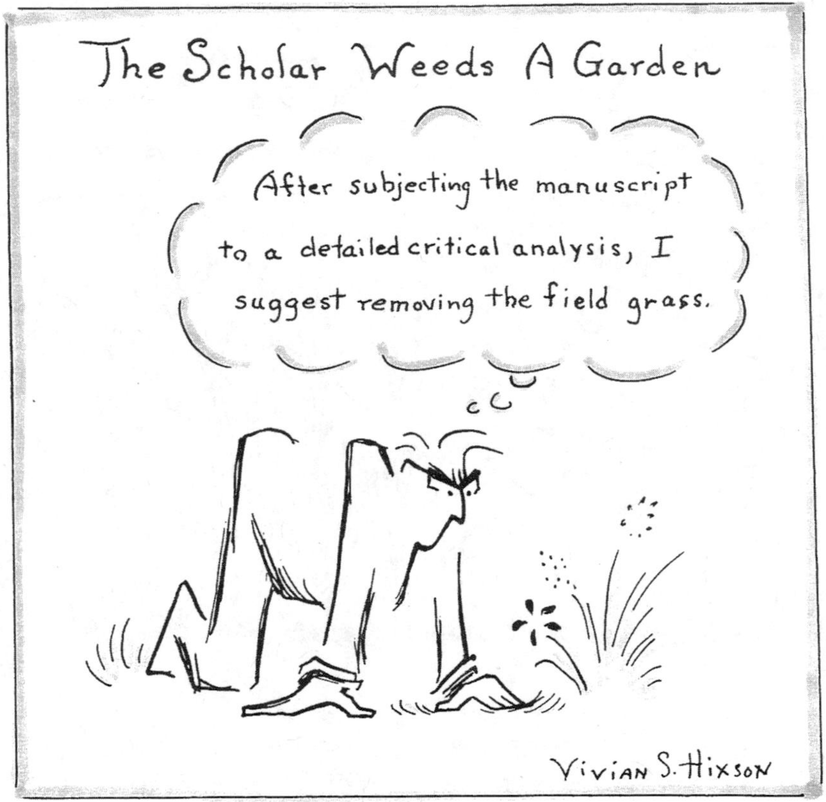
The Scholar Weeds A Garden
After subjecting the manuscript to a detailed critical analysis, I suggest removing the field grass.
Vivian S. Hixson

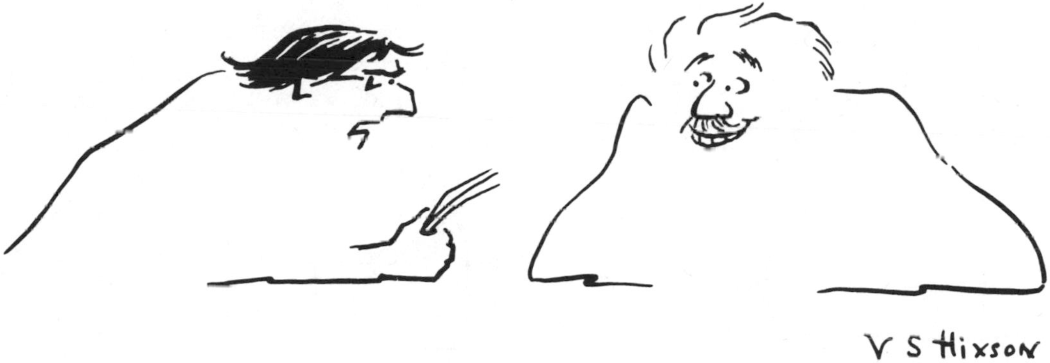
V S Hixson

"I'll put your research paper in my session on one condition. You can*not* turn around and walk out right after you give it. If we have to listen to *your* presentation, you have to listen to *ours*."

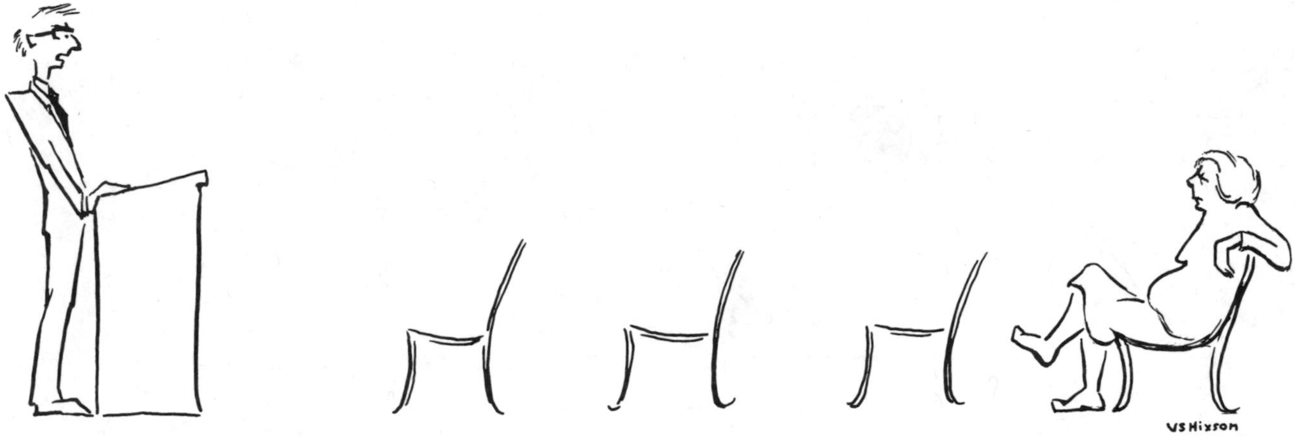
VS Hixson

First paper.

"All right, so it's depressing, obscure, and unreadable. The real question is, will they accept it as a dissertation?"

"I've got it! I'll start a new journal that will publish your stuff, and you'll start a new journal that will publish *my* stuff, and we'll both get tenure!"

The Origin of Species, Chapter III.

"Well, yes, I should say your book probably *is* the last word on the subject!"

"I'm not sure, but I did notice that there was a letter from a publisher in his box."

"How do you do. I am the misinformed sycophant you referred to on page 96."

"Look, Joe, they cited your article! You're on your way to becoming an important footnote!"

"So you've finished the Sistine Chapel. Great! Now what's your *next* project?"

"I'm not going to apply to just *any* college. It's got to be in a warm climate, and it's got to have good-looking girls."

"How about football/basketball/track/drama/student council with a 2.0 GPA?
Or would you prefer the leader of an all-girl rock band with a 1.5?"

"I know he's not a scholar, and he's never going to be one. But isn't there room in this college for somebody who's going to have a couple of million dollars to throw around?"

"No, no, you've got it wrong! When the parents are along, you do the library tour, the classroom tour. When you've got the students *alone* you do the video games and the bars."

"I started out in English, and then I went into gerontology, and then for two semesters I was into biology, but what I really want is a physics major. Is there any way I can do that and graduate next semester?"

"What I'd really like is a job that doesn't take a lot of time and energy but pays a lot of money so I can be truly creative on my own time."

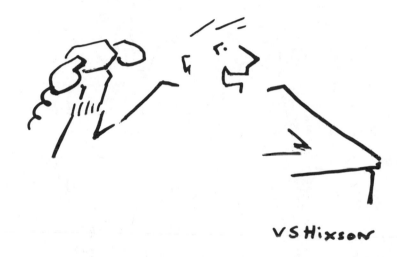

"OK! My roommate's bringing a tape deck, a hi-fi, a microwave, and a refrigerator, and I'm bringing my TV. If I can just get a VCR, my first year at college will be great!"

VS Hixson

"We were standing in the grocery store line, just talking, you know?
And I looked around, and there was this *professor* standing behind us!"

"So your basic thesis is that some colleges have an anti-intellectual student subculture?"

"We're going to be throwing an all-night big-bash party, and hey,
if the noise bothers you, why don't you just come over and join us?"

"Oh, I love living in a college town! When the students are gone, of course."

"I told my son that we didn't have the money to send him to college *and* buy him a car,
and he would just have to decide which one would be really more important
in the long run. I think that was a mistake."

"Jim? This is your Mom! It's so great to hear your voice again! Say, do you have just a few minutes to talk before your next class? We have a little problem . . ."

"Hey, if I leave the first campus at ten o'clock sharp, drive eighty miles per hour to Centerville, get out of there at noon and turbo down to State by two P.M., I can take on enough of these part-time teaching jobs to pay the rent!"

"Congratulations! You have just been appointed assistant professor! We'll expect you
to teach three courses, sit on four committees, grade four hundred papers,
and turn out at least one original article each term."

"You'll be teaching Explorations in Contemporary Literary Thought and Critical Exposition in the Twentieth Century. Actually, they're two sections of Remedial Freshman Comp."

"I've got it! I'll take half of my first course, add half of my second course, and bingo! I've got my third course!"

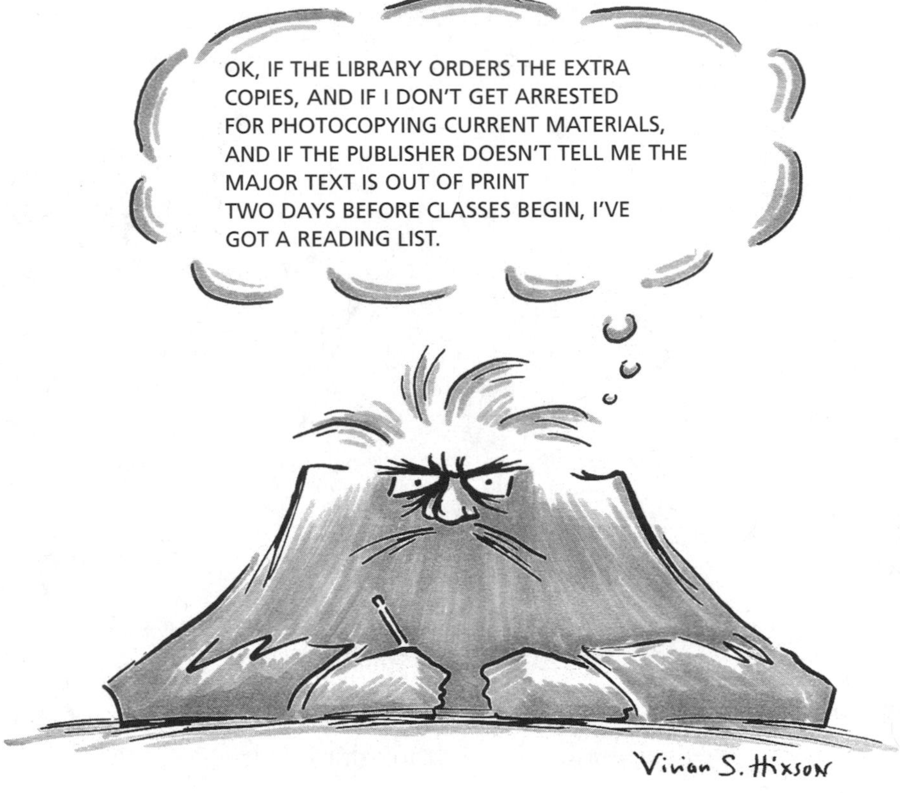
OK, IF THE LIBRARY ORDERS THE EXTRA COPIES, AND IF I DON'T GET ARRESTED FOR PHOTOCOPYING CURRENT MATERIALS, AND IF THE PUBLISHER DOESN'T TELL ME THE MAJOR TEXT IS OUT OF PRINT TWO DAYS BEFORE CLASSES BEGIN, I'VE GOT A READING LIST.
Vivian S. Hixson

"I realize he hasn't written anything himself, but his course pack selections are brilliant."

"This is the best reading list I've ever developed; there's nothing in it that's still under copyright!"

VS Hixson

"I've been assigned to the Curriculum Reform Committee, and so I thought I'd read up on it, but I can't seem to find any records of any actual meetings. Am I looking in the wrong place?"

The History Department debates the new curriculum.

"The Dean has just decided that the true mission of this department is not research but undergraduate teaching. . . . Did I say something wrong?"

"For God's sake, be realistic! If we don't admit three more people to the graduate
program, we'll be three paper graders short!"

Vivian S. Hixson

The perfect class.

"But Professor, according to the new university guidelines, this *is* a small class."

"Why yes, I do think I remember you. Weren't you in that class in the football stadium?"

"It's Representative Brundle. He wants to know why we're not hard at work in the classroom."

"He's going to ask to audit your course. For God's sake, don't let him. It used to be *his* course."

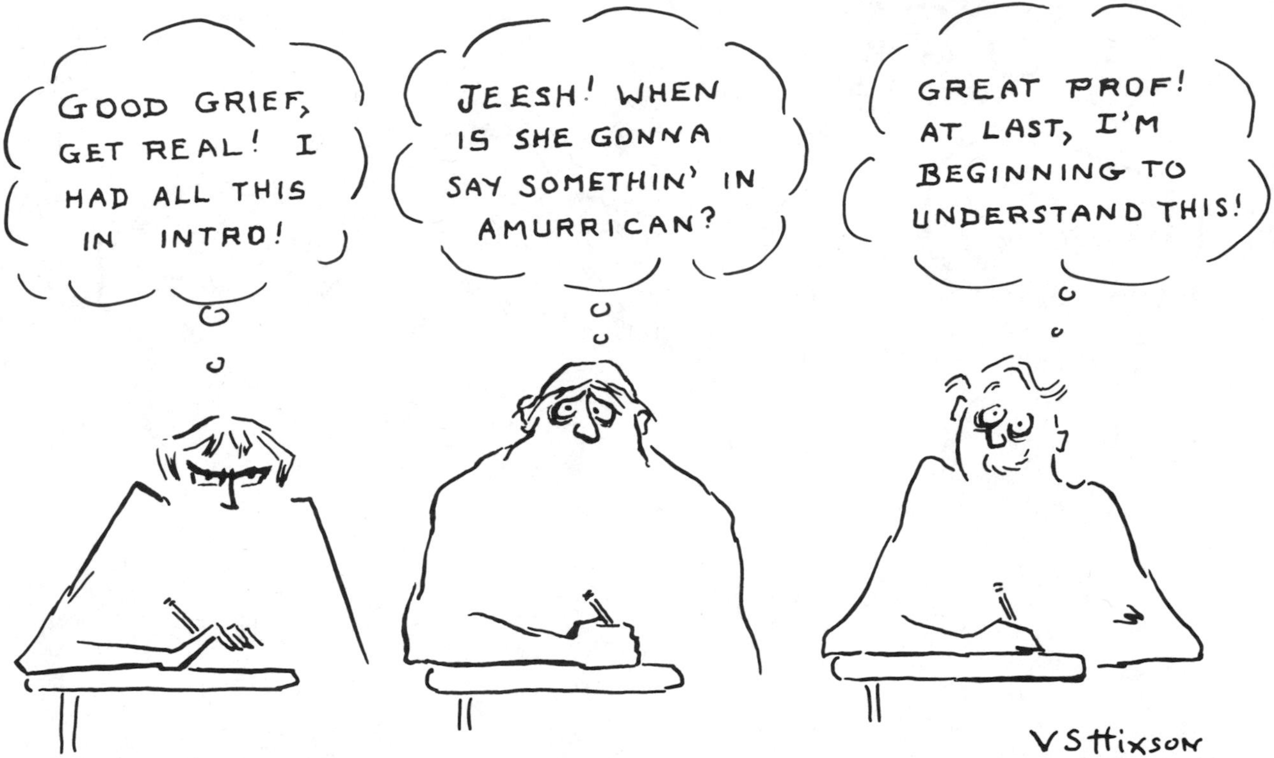
GOOD GRIEF, GET REAL! I HAD ALL THIS IN INTRO!
JEESH! WHEN IS SHE GONNA SAY SOMETHIN' IN AMURRICAN?
GREAT PROF! AT LAST, I'M BEGINNING TO UNDERSTAND THIS!
VSHixson

"Yeah, I've got American History this term. But hey, no sweat, I've lived in America all my life."

"None of that wishy-washy relativism in *this* seminar!"

VS Hixson

View from the lectern of class containing seventy-five students and one six-month-old baby.

"So the last I saw of them was when they had decided that the classroom was too hot and they were moving the class outdoors."

"You know, I'm beginning to wonder if this prof is really used to teaching an eight o'clock class."

"I'm going to have to miss class next week; you won't be doing anything important, will you?"

"Actually, I liked the students I used to get at the community college better than the ones I get here at the university, but for God's sake, don't tell anybody I said that."

VSHixson

"Ok, I'll give the same lecture again, and this time,
pretend you're a right-wing Republican from Texas."

V S Hixson

"I was born at the wrong time. As soon as I was far enough
along to *expect* deference, deference went out of style."

"Hey, don't worry! They can't throw you out. You came here, you paid your tuition, you took all those courses. . . . They *owe* you a Ph.D."

"For this class, I think I'll make the average grade a 3.0. A 3.0 says, 'I do have *some* standards, but, hey, I'm really a nice guy.'"

"Look, Harvey, the only reason you're depressed is that you're letting yourself be bound by conventional standards. *I* think that writing 5,383 multiple-choice questions *is* a contribution to literature."

"Term papers are a snap. Just write a great first couple of pages.
They'll never get around to reading the rest of it."

"No, wait! Not this week! If we're going to have a baby, it *has* to be born in June, *after* I've finished grading papers!"

"Now that the semester is over, I just want to say that it's been wonderful getting to know all of you."

DREAMS OF ACADEMIC GLORY

VStlixson

Thrilled by the last lecture, the class rises in spontaneous applause.

Quick Guide to the Cartoons

Meetings and Committees 1

Administration 9

Finances 22

Buildings and Grounds 31

Grants and Research 37

Writing, Presenting, and Publishing 59

Recruiting and Advising Students 77

Students, Parents, and the College Town 83

Teaching: Hiring the Staff, Revising the Curriculum, Planning the Courses 90

Teaching: Lecturing, Discussing, Testing, Grading, and the Last Class 101

Vivian Scott Hixson

Vivian Scott Hixson is the creator of hundreds of cartoons published by the *Chronicle of Higher Education*. She is currently Adjunct Assistant Professor of Sociology at Michigan State University.

David L. Lendt is the author of *Ding: The Life of Jay Norwood Darling*, an award-winning biography of the Pulitzer Prize–winning political cartoonist and conservationist.

LIBRARY
ST. LOUIS COMMUNITY COLLEGE
AT FLORISSANT VALLEY